'Ferocious Frankie' of the 361st Fighter Group, 374th Fighter Squadron, 8th Air Force, ETO.

NORTH AMERICAN P-51D MUSTANG
IN USAAF·USAF SERVICE

Illustrated & compiled by Richard Ward

ACKNOWLEDGEMENTS

This pictorial survey of one of the most famous fighter aircraft of World War II could not have been published without the generous assistance of many friends whose names are arranged below in alphabetical order . . . my thanks to all;

Ray E. Bowers, Peter M. Bowers, Jos. F. Consiglio, Roger A. Freeman, George J. Letzter, Ernest R. McDowell, David W. Menard, Frank F. Smith. Acknowledgement is also due to the Ministry of Defence and last but not least the United States Air Force.

'Sigh!' P-51D. Possibly of 5th or 6th Fighter Sqdn. 1st Air Commando Group, 10th Air Force, CBI.

PUBLISHED BY

Arco Publishing Company, Inc., 219 Park Avenue South, New York, N.Y. 10003

First Published by Osprey Publications Ltd. and Printed in Great Britain

Library of Congress No. 76-87227 · Library Edition SBN 668-02094-6 · Paperback Edition SBN 668-02093-8

AIRCAM AVIATION SERIES

Each publication illustrates one type or major sub-types of a famous aircraft in the colour schemes and markings of the Air Forces of the World. Each issue will contain eight pages of colour side view illustrations, supporting black and white plan view drawings showing where necessary both upper and under surfaces, one hundred and twenty-five half-tone photographs, each issue will also contain one full colour plate illustrating twenty examples of Unit Insignia of the World's Air Forces.

No. 1 **NORTH AMERICAN P-51D MUSTANG IN USAAF-USAF SERVICE.**

No. 2 **REPUBLIC P-47 THUNDERBOLT.** In USAAF-USAF; RAF; Free French; French Air Force; Mexican, Brazilian and other Air Forces.

No. 3 **NORTH AMERICAN MUSTANG Mk. I-IV.** In RAF; RAAF; SAAF; RNZAF; RCAF service and the **NORTH AMERICAN P-51B and D MUSTANG** in French; Italian; Swedish; Royal Netherlands; Netherlands East Indies; Indonesian; Israeli; Philippine; Dominican; Somali; South Korean; Chinese Nationalist; Chinese Communist, etc., Air Forces.

No. 4 **SUPERMARINE SPITFIRE Mk. I-XVI, MERLIN ENGINE.** In RAF; RAAF; SAAF; RCAF; USAAF; Belgian; Polish; Czechoslovakian; Free French; French; R. Norwegian; R. Netherlands; R. Danish; Israeli; Italian; Greek; Turkish; Portuguese; Egyptian; Burmese, etc., Air Forces.

No. 5 **NORTH AMERICAN P-51B/C MUSTANG IN USAAF SERVICE.** Similar content to No. 1 but with brief coverage of the P-51 and A-36.

No. 6 **CURTISS (P-40) KITTYHAWK Mk. I-IV.** In RAF; RAAF; RNZAF; SAAF; RCAF; Netherlands East Indies; Russian and Finnish Air Forces. The Curtis P-40 Warhawk will be covered in a future issue.

SPECIFICATION

North American P-51D Mustang

Dimensions: Span 37 ft. 05/16 in.; Length 32 ft. 3¼ in.; Height 13 ft. 8 in.; Wing area 233·19 sq. ft.

Weights: Empty 7,125 lb.; Normal loaded 10,000 lb.; Maximum weight (489 gallons of fuel) 11,600 lb.

Performance: Maximum speed at 25,000 ft. - 437 m.p.h.; 15,000 ft. - 413 m.p.h.; 5,000 ft. - 395 m.p.h.; Cruising 362 m.p.h.; Landing speed 100 m.p.h.; Ceiling 41,000 ft.; Climb rate 3,475 ft. per min.; Range normal 950 miles; Maximum with 489 gallons of fuel 2,290 miles.

Power unit: Packard Rolls-Royce Merlin V-1650-7 developing 1,450 h.p. at take-off, 1,650 h.p. under combat emergency conditions.

Armament: 6 × ·50 in. Browning MG 53-2 machine guns; 2 × 1,000 lb. bombs; 10 × 5 in. HV aircraft rockets.

Price: $51,000 approx.

P-51D of the yellow nosed 361st Fighter Group, 8th Air Force bombed-up and ready to go on a dawn op. Little Walden, Herts. (USAF)

NORTH AMERICAN P-51D MUSTANG

If a list of the dozen most outstanding military aircraft of the century is compiled in the year 2,000, there is little doubt that the North American P-51 Mustang will be included. The finest American fighter of the Second World War, and one of the classic fighters of all time, the Mustang was the fruit more of a happy series of chances than a deliberately evolved policy.

It was born in response to a request from the British Purchasing Commission in the United States for a P-40 replacement. The early model P-51's and P-51A's, first delivered to the R.A.F. in mid-1942, were useful ground attack aircraft by virtue of their armament of four 0.5 in. and four 0.3 in. machine guns; but the low altitude rating of their Allison engines rendered them unsuitable for normal fighter operations. It was not until a British suggestion led to the mating of the excellent Mustang airframe with the classic Rolls-Royce Merlin engine that the full potential of the type became apparent.

The U.S.A.A.F. in England received their first P-51B's and P-51C's powered by Packard-built Merlins in December 1943; and during that month they carried out their first mission in the rôle which will always be the Mustang's main claim to immortality — long range bomber escort.

The cleaned-up P-51D, with a more powerful engine and the rear vision immeasurably improved by a new "bubble" canopy, was delivered to the U.S.A.A.F. fighter squadrons in Europe and the Pacific in 1944; and it proved to be the definitive version of the design. The most important advantage held by the Mustang over its contemporaries was range, and thus its ability to accompany the B-17 Flying Fortresses and B-24 Liberators of the U.S. 8th Bomber Command on their deep penetration raids from England over Germany and occupied Europe. The daylight bombing offensive had up to that time extracted a high cost in American lives; the fighter types previously available to the Allies had been able to do little more than take the bombers half way to their target, and then sortie again to meet the survivors and shepherd them home over the Channel. For the critical hours immediately before and after reaching the target area, the bombers had to withstand as best they could the attacks of the determined and magnificently brave German fighter pilots of the Home Defence organization. Now, at last, the Allies had a first-class fighter aircraft capable of accompany-

---

Front cover captions from top to bottom:
88 of the 325th Fighter Group, 319th Fighter Squadron, 15th Air Force, Italy
' Horses Itch ' flown by Maj. Hiro, 357th Fighter Group, 363rd Fighter Squadron, 8th Air Force, ETO
' Moonbeam McSwine ' flown by Capt. William Whishner, 352nd Fighter Group, 487th Fighter Squadron, 8th Air Force, ETO
F-51D of the Pennsylvania Air National Guard
F-51D of the West Virginia Air National Guard, see photo

20th FG, 55th FS, dispersal area at Kingscliffe, Northants. P-51D's showing 20th FG early style nose marking and OD fuselage top decking and wing upper surfaces. (via G. J. Letzter)

ing the bombers on the 1,100 mile round trip to Berlin.

Jettisoning almost-empty drop tanks, the P-51's could meet the Messerschmitts and Focke-Wulfs of the Reichsverteidigung on equal terms. Although rather vulnerable to fire from the 20 mm. and 30 mm. cannon which most Luftwaffe fighters carried, the P-51D was superior in speed and manoeuvrability to all German piston-engined fighters over 20,000 feet, which was the normal altitude of the escorted bomber formations.

The improvement in the efficiency and morale of the bomber force was incalculable; the squadrons of Mustangs weaving and darting around the Fortress phalanxes were an ever-present reassurance to the crews that their lonely crucifixion was over. Apart from the direct results of the continued American bombardment of the German aircraft and armament industry, the added strain imposed on the Luftwaffe fighter units was proportionately massive. Already suffering from the conflicting demands on its resources from Russia, Italy and the West, the German fighter arm now faced a rapid increase in losses over the homeland. It had been a formidable enough task to make an impression on the massed guns of the Fortress and Liberator formations; now every interceptor mission involved the risk of meeting modern fighter aircraft determined to keep the interceptors from their charges, and frequently with a considerable height advantage. The bomber crews had good reason for the affection they soon formed for their " Little Friends."

The P-51D was not used solely in the escort rôle, however. As the numbers of Mustang squadrons increased, and the air war over Europe began to tilt inexorably in favour of the Allies, the P-51's joined the mighty P-47D Thunderbolts of the 9th U.S. Air Force and the Spitfires and Typhoons of R.A.F. Fighter Command, in a calculated effort to win total air superiority over the coasts earmarked for the

opening of the Second Front. By keeping up an unrelenting pressure on the seriously depleted German fighter defences along the coast of Hitler's Festung Europa, the Allied air forces won the initiative; and then began the " softening-up " of German forces in France and the Low Countries in preparation for the invasion. The Mustang was responsible for the destruction of vast numbers of vehicles and installations along the invasion coast during the build-up before D-Day, and the period of the actual landings. By the time the Allied armies broke out of the Normandy beachheads and began to strike south and east, the P-51D and its stable-mates had won such total command of the skies over the battlefront that all German road and rail traffic by day was in constant danger of destruction. As the air war over Europe continued, and resistance to the Allied bombing offensive was pushed back by the advance of the ground forces, a proportion of the escort formations of Mustangs would leave their " Big Friends " when they were safely on their way back to England, and indulge in " free chase " operations over the fighting front and the German rear echelons. These marauding operations rose to such a pitch in the last months of the war that by the Spring of 1945, any sort of daylight movement by German troops was an invitation to instant attack from the air. During ground-attack missions, the P-51D was frequently fitted with racks for rocket projectiles, in addition to the standard armament of six 0.5 in. machine guns with 1,260 rounds of ammunition.

As well as escorting the bombers on their normal round-trip raids over Germany, the far-ranging P-51D's accompanied the " shuttle " raids, deep penetration attacks flown from the U.S.A.A.F. bases in England, which continued east or south after striking the target and landed on airfields in Russia or North Africa. With an 85 U.S. gallon fuselage tank and two 92 gallon wing cells, the Mustang had a normal range of 1,300 miles; two 75 or 150 gallon drop tanks could also be carried.

P-51D, 20th FG, 77th FS, 8th AF, upper surfaces camouflaged OD. ' Its the Kid ' port and stbd. in black. No wing bands. (USAF)

The Mustang flew in three other theatres of operations besides Northern Europe. In the Mediterranean, P-51D's of the U.S. 15th Air Force operated in support of the British and American armies in the last months of the gruelling Italian campaign. They escorted Fortresses and Liberators on trips to the Ploesti oil refineries in Rumania; and, together with many other Allied fighter types, added to the problems of the German forces in the Balkans.

In the China-Burma-India theatre the P-51's played their part in harassing the Japanese armies and disrupting their communications. Over the vast areas of the Pacific war zone their range was an ideal asset. After the capture of Iwo Jima in February 1945, the P-51D's began to operate alongside the B-29 Superfortresses of the U.S. 20th Bomber Command in their long-range offensive against the Japanese Home Islands. They made the first land-based fighter strike against Tokyo, on April 7th, 1945. With external tanks fitted the P-51D had a total capacity of 489 U.S. gallons, giving it the remarkable range of 2,080 miles, and an endurance of $8\frac{1}{2}$ hours in the air!

The versatility of the design also allowed conversion for reconnaissance duties; designated F-6D in this rôle, the Mustang carried vertical and oblique cameras and additional radio gear.

Probably the outstanding P-51 unit in Northern Europe was the 4th Fighter Group, led by Colonel Don Blakeslee. Formed round a nucleus of ex-R.A.F. "Eagle Squadron" pilots, the Group was based at Debden, and numbered among its officers several of the outstanding American fighter pilots of the war. Some of these pilots have become household words — Don Gentile, John Godfrey, Ralph Hofer, Nicholas Megura, Duane Beason; and throughout their operations they maintained a friendly rivalry with the Thunderbolt pilots of the other premier American fighter group, the 56th — "Hub Zemke's Wolfpack."

The red-nosed P-51's of the 4th Group took part in all the major battles of the daylight offensive. They made many sorties to Berlin, and were in the forefront of the calculated campaign of bringing the Luftwaffe to combat, and destroying them, on every possible occasion. On D-Day, along with the other 8th Air Force fighter groups, they provided a wall of fighters round the American beachheads, sealing the area off from the expected Luftwaffe onslaught which never

materialised. Two weeks later the 4th provided the escort for an American "shuttle" raid; and after $7\frac{1}{2}$ hours in the air, landed at Piryatin within one minute of the estimated arrival time. Of the group's 68 Mustangs, one had been shot down over Germany, the second (Ralph Hofer's "Salem Representative") was off on a private war, eventually landing safely at Kiev. By the end of the European war, the 4th had destroyed 1,016 German aircraft. The top scorers were Maj. John Godfrey (36), Maj. Don Gentile (33) and Maj. Duane Beeson (25)*

Top scorer in the U.S. 9th Air Force was Lt. Bruce Carr, who ended the war with 14 victories and $11\frac{1}{2}$ enemy aircraft destroyed on the ground. This 354th F.G. pilot, whose P-51D was christened "Angel's Playmate," was one of two American fighter pilots who became "aces in a day." This apparent contradiction in terms comes about through the American system under which any pilot who destroys five enemy aircraft is dubbed an ace; and on 2nd April 1945 Carr shot down three Fw 190's and two Bf 109's.

Mainly the Mustangs of the 9th Air Force were employed on ground attack, in line with the tactical rôle of the parent organization; however, towards the end of the war such distinctions became blurred, all Mustangs attacking any target which presented itself, in the air or on the ground.

Operating from Lesina air field in Italy, the most famous Southern European group was the 325th — "The Checkertails." They relinquished their P-47's for P-51B's and P-51C's in May 1944, and began receiving P-51D's shortly afterwards. Their war mainly consisted of fighter sweeps and escort missions, and their hunting-grounds were Italy, Southern France, Austria, Germany, Hungary, Czechoslovakia and Rumania. They made many escort sorties with the "Big Friends," notably the frequent attacks on the Rumanian oil installations; and many fighter sweeps over German airfields and transport facilities in Eastern Europe. They also had a chance to try

---

*These scores, in the usual American fashion, include aircraft destroyed on the ground. The actual aerial victories were: Godfrey (18), Gentile (23), Beeson (18) and the whole Group, 550. By European custom the 56th F.G., with 680 kills in aerial combat, would be considered the winners of the Group race.

'Gentle Annie,' P-51D of the 20th FG, 79th FS, 8th AF, showing early 20th FG black and white nose marking, photo taken at Bottisham during Group Commanders conference. (USAF)

'Sad Sack' of the 20th FG, 77th FS, 8th AF, showing later black and white 20th Group nose marking. Black disc tail marking. (via G. J. Letzter)

their hand at "shuttle" raiding to Russia, and long escort missions from Italy to Berlin and back. The 325th's leading Mustang aces were Capt. Harry Parker (13) and Capt. Wayne Lowry (11). The Group's 319th Squadron numbered among its officers one particularly distinctive pilot — a Lt. Hiawatha Mohawk!

The first Mustang units in the Pacific theatre were the machines of the 15th and 21st Fighter Groups, shipped from Hawaii to Saipan in February and on to Iwo Jima in March of 1945. The first few weeks of operations were spent in attacks on ground targets in the Bonin Islands; but on April 7th 96 P-51D's from the two Groups escorted the B-29's of the 20th Bomber Command on a trip which they were to repeat many times in the next four months — the

round trip to Tokyo. Although the 1,500 mile mission allowed only about a quarter of an hour's loiter over the target, the two Groups shot down 21 Japanese interceptors for the loss of two Mustangs.

The 15th and 21st were joined in May by the 506th Fighter Group, and continued to alternate escort missions with ground attack operations until the end of the war. The 506th took part in one particularly grim episode, on the 1st June, when 15 P-51D's and 12 pilots were lost — but not to enemy action. They are presumed to have run out of fuel after encountering severe weather on the return trip, a pointed reminder of the risks of flying over the immense Pacific combat area, even in the far-ranging Mustang.

P-51D UNITS

The major units equipped with the P-51D in the various theatres of operations included the following:

8th A.F., E.T.O.	78th F.G.	354th F.G.	359th F.G.
4th F.G.	339th F.G.	355th F.G.	361st F.G.
20th F.G.	352nd F.G.	356th F.G.	364th F.G.
	353rd F.G.	357th F.G.	379th F.G.
9th A.F., E.T.O.	354th F.G.	370th F.G.	67th T.R.G.
	363rd F.G.	10th P.R.G.	69th T.R.G.
15th A.F., ITALY	31st F.G.	325th F.G.	68th T.R.G.
	52nd F.G.	332nd F.G.	
10th A.F., C.B.I.	23rd F.G.	311th F.G.	1st, 2nd Air Commando
	51st F.G.	8th P.R.G.	
5th A.F., S.W.P.A.	8th F.G. (P.W.)	71st P.R.G.	3rd Air Commando
7th A.F./20th A.F., P.O.A.			
15th F.G.	21st F.G.	35th F.G.	506th F.G.
3rd A.F., U.S. (T)	53rd F.G.	337th F.G.	407th F.G.
	54th F.G.	338th F.G.	
4th A.F., U.S. (T)	369th F.G.	372nd F.G.	

Abbreviations: E.T.O.—European Theatre of Operations; C.B.I. — China - Burma - India Theatre; P.O.A.—Pacific Operational Area; (P.W.)—Post war; (T) — Training; F.G. — Fighter Group; P.R.G. — Photographic Reconnaisance Group; T.R.G. — Tactical Reconnaisance Group.

P-51D's of the 20th FG, 55th FS, 8th AF taxying round the perimeter track at Kingscliffe prior to take-off for an escort mission over Germany. (via G. J. Letzter)

P.51D, 20th FG, 79th FS, 8th AF, 'Dolly' in yellow outlined black. No wing bands.

Right. MC-R 'Bridgets Bunnion' 20th FG, 79th FS, 8th AF. Capt. Darrel A. Beschen's a/c flown by Capt. Robert H. Pollock.

Below. Black nose markings only on 'Little Lady,' red outlined white. 20th FG, 55th FS, 8th AF. (USAF)

P-51D, 359th FG, 370th FS, 8th AF, flown by Maj. Ray S. Kenman, 24½ destroyed. Green nose, blue rudder. (via G. J. Letzter)

'Hubert' green nosed red ruddered P-51D of the 359th FG, 369th FS, 8th AF, flown by F/Lt. R. L. Burtner. (via G. J. Letzter)

P-51D, 359th FG, 368th FS, 8th AF, green nose, yellow rudder. Eight swastikas under the cockpit, pilot unknown. (via G. J. Letzter)

Line up of 359th FG, 368th FS, 8th AF, P-51's at East Wretham, Norfolk. Green noses, yellow rudders, five black crosses on canopy frame of 'Lady,' second a/c in line. (via G. J. Letzter)

Formation of 356th FG, 361st FS, 8th AF, P-51D's returning from escort mission to Lutzkendorf, Germany, 9th Feb. 1945. (USAF)

Blue and white nosed P-51D of the 364th FG, 383rd FS, 8th AF, Honnington, Suffolk, May 1945. Note rocket attachment points under wing. (USAF)

Above. P-51D, 364th FG, 385th FS, 8th AF, in rough country. 'Rugged Rebel' in black, note twin rear-view mirrors. Honnington. (USAF)

Left. P-51D probably of the 1st Scouting Force, 1st Bomb. Division, 8th AF. Red/white nose, red tail trim, OD canopy frame. (via G. J. Letzter)

Below. P-51D, 352nd FG, 486th FS, 8th AF, after belly landing at Manston, Kent. Blue nose, yellow rudder. (Ray E. Bowers)

' Paddy II ' of the 352nd FG, 328th FS, 8th AF, dispersed at Bodney, Norfolk, ETO. (USAF)

' Moonbeam McSwine ' of the blue-nosed 352nd FG, flown by Maj. William Wishner, 15 victories, of the 487th FS, 8th AF, Bodney, Norfolk, ETO. (USAF)

' Straw Boss 2 ' of the 352nd FG, 328th FS, 8th AF. Photo taken at Bottisham during Group Commanders conference. (USAF)

P-51D, 4th FG, 334th FS, 8th AF. Photo taken at Manston after emergency landing. (Ray E. Bowers)

P-51D, 355th FG, 354th FS, 8th AF. ' Bulldogs ' above exhaust ports ' Jane II ' below, flown by Col. Marshall. (via G. J. Letzter)

Above. ' Faithful Fernie II,' 355th FG, 354th FS, 8th AF. Red/nat. metal/red nose and rudder. Name in black (via Jos. F. Consiglio)

P-51D, 355th FG, 354th FS, 8th AF. See colour illustration. (USAF)

Blue nose band and rudder on this P-51D of the 355th FG, 357th FS, 8th AF. Note white 472 on rudder. (via Frank F. Smith)

P-51D flown by Capt. Minchew, 355th FG, 357th FS, 8th AF. Seven black crosses on canopy. (via G. J. Letzter)

Yellow nosed P-51D, 361st FG, 374th FS, 8th AF. 'Ferocious Frankie' in black, five black crosses on OD panel on canopy frame. Note D-Day Invasion stripes have been overpainted on upper surface of wings. (USAF)

Two 361st FG, P-51D's in formation with a P-51B over France. (USAF)

Magnificent shot of yellow nosed, medium blue camouflaged P-51D of the 361st FG, 375th FS, 8th AF. (USAF)

P-51D of the 361st FG, 374th FS, 8th AF. Photo taken on ops. over France, pilot Lt.-Col. Roy A. Webb. (USAF)

Yellow nose and ruddered P-51D of the 361st FG, 376th FS, 8th AF, over France. Note additional thin black stripe to D-Day identification markings. (USAF)

P-51D's of the 361st FG, 375th FS, 8th AF. Yellow noses medium blue camouflage. 'Lou IV' flown by Col. J. J. Christian who was killed in this a/c while dive bombing a target in France in 1944. A/c 'A' 'Skybouncer.' (USAF)

'Yakima Chief,' P-51D of the 479th FG, 434th FS, 8th AF. Highly polished spinner and red rudder. Note serial has been deleted.

Buffed spinner and yellow ruddered P-51D of the 479th FG, 435th FS, 8th AF, touching down at Wattisham, Suffolk, home base of the 479th FG. Code is J2-.
(Ray E. Bowers)

P-51D of the same unit coming in at Wattisham. Note greyed in national insignia. 479th FG used polished spinner only as nose marking.

'Weezy,' black ruddered P-51D of the 479th FG, 436th FS, 8th AF, off the runway at Manston. A/c letter and serial unknown.
(Ray E. Bowers)

'The Millie P,' one of many similarly named Mustangs flown by Maj. Gillier, 55th FG, 343rd FS, 8th AF, operating from Wormingford, Northants. (Ministry of Defence)

P-51D, 55th FG, 343rd FS, 8th AF, ' Miss Marilyn II ' in similar scheme to the ' Millie P ' but without tail stripes. (via G. J. Letzter)

'The Bengal Lancer,' a P-51D of the 339th FG, 503rd FS, 8th AF, taxying through winter snow at Fowlmere, Cambridge, January 1945. (USAF)

'Roller,' a P-51D of the 339th FG, 504th FS, 8th AF at rest in marshland, near Manston, Kent. Emergency and bad weather airfield. (Ray E. Bowers)

P-51D, 339th FG, 505th FS, also at rest at Manston. (Ray E. Bowers)

504th FS Mustang coming in to land at Fowlmere, Cambs. March 1945. (USAF)

P-51D 'Mary' of the 339th FG, 505th FS. 8th AF, flown by Lt. Baugher. Red and white nose, yellow rudder. Note unusual position of code, 5Q, under port wing. (USAF)

Mount of an Ace, 'Pauline,' flown by Lt. Jos. Thury, 12½ e.a. destroyed. 339th FG, 504th FS, 8th AF. Note twin rear-view mirrors. Serial 414656. (USAF)

Close formation of P-51D's of the 353rd FG, 350th FS, 8th AF. Yellow rudders. (USAF)

'Willit Run?' taxying in at Raydon, Suffolk, after returning from a mission over Europe. 353rd FG, 351st FS, 8th AF. (USAF)

'Danny Boy 2nd' belly down in the frost. Serial 415516, name repeated on port side. 353rd FG, 350th FS, 8th AF. Dec. 1944. (USAF)

'Ginny,' 353rd FG, 351st FS, 8th AF. Code YJ, serial 414706. Wing bands outlined in white. (via G. J. Letzter)

'Butch 3rd' somewhat butchered after crash landing at Raydon, Suffolk, base of the 353rd FG. A/c belongs to the 351st FS, 8th AF. July 1945. (USAF)

'Dallas Doll" of the 353rd FG, 352nd FS, 8th AF, standing ready in dispersal area at Raydon, Suffolk. Note early compressed paper long-range tank. (USAF)

P-51D's of the 353rd rolling along the perimeter track prior to taking off. Dec. 1944. (USAF)

350th FS, P-51D landing at Raydon after escort mission. Feb. 1945. (USAF)

'Donna-Mite' of the 352nd FS coming in at Raydon, serial 411624. Feb. 1945. (USAF)

A pair of 352nd FS, P-51D's lined up ready to take off on op. Raydon. Dec. 1944. (USAF)

'Stasia II' of the 353rd FG, 352nd FS, 8th AF. Black and yellow checks on nose. Raydon. Dec. 1944. (USAF)

P-51D 'Double Trouble two' of the 353rd FG, 352nd FS, 8th AF. Note yellow outline to code letter s. (USAF)

Nose detail of 350th FS Mustang 'Baby-Duck' flown by Capt. Kolb. (USAF)

Tight formation of 357th FG, 362nd FS, 8th AF, P-51D's. 1st a/c 'Sweet Helen II.' 2nd a/c 'Wee Willy' 413334, Capt. Harvey Mace. 3rd a/c G4-G 413719. 4th a/c 'Bow Legs' 413596, 1st Lt. Coon. (via Ernest Vagi)

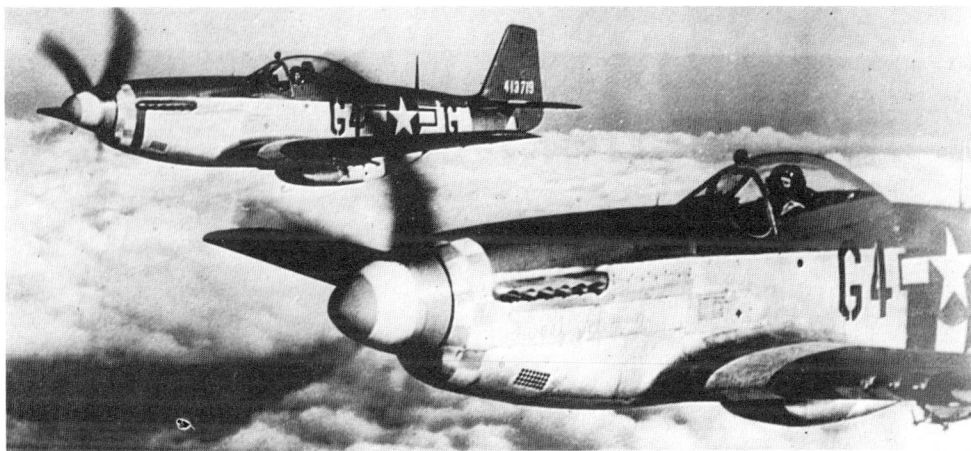

Two P-51D's of the same formation above. (via Ernest Vagi)

Nose of G4-G of the 357th FG, 362 FS, 8th AF. (via Ernest Vagi)

Nose detail of Capt. Bochkay's P-51D. White wings, black Club and detail. (P. Yant via C. J. Letzter)

P-51D of the 357th FG, 362nd FS, 8th AF, on taxi track at Leiston, Norfolk. June 1945. (USAF)

P-51D 'Hurry Home Honey,' 357th FG, 364th FS, 8th AF, flown by Cpt. Richard A. Peterson, CO of the 364th FS, escorting flak-crippled B-17 Fortress home from Germany. Photo taken from B-17 by Cpl. E. W. Poveroff. (USAF)

'Tangerine,' 357th FG, 364th FS, flown by Cpt. Richard A. Peterson, 15 victories. CO of the 364th FS. 'Tangerine' in orange. (USAF)

'Horses Itch' flown by Maj. Hiro of the 357th FG, 363rd FS, 8th AF. Code B6-D, serial 413518. White nose. (via G. J. Letzter)

Close formation of P-51D's of the 357th FG, 364th FS, 8th AF. (via G. J. Letzter)

P-51D of the 357th FG, 363rd FS, 8th AF, on dispersal area, Leiston, Norfolk. (via Fred C. Dickey)

463177, MX-C of the 78th FG, 82nd FS, 8th AF, pranged at Duxford, Cambs. Jan. 1945.

'Small Boy Here' of the 78th FG, 83rd FS, 8th AF, also pranged at Duxford. May 1945.

Above. P-51D of the 78th FG, 84th FS, crash-landed at Duxford. June 1945.

Below. 415699 also bent at Duxford. 78th FG, 84th FS, 8th AF. Jan. 1945. (USAF)

Line-up of 78th FG, MX- 82nd FS, 83rd FS- to left.

Above. From left to right 84th, 83rd, 82nd FS's of the 78th FG, 8th AF. All photos taken June 1945 at Duxford.

Below. 78th FG, 84th FS, black rudders: 83rd FS, white outlined red rudders; 82nd FS, red rudders, all spinners halved black/white. (USAF)

A

1
P-51D, 20th Fighter Group, 55th Fighter Squadron, 8th Air Force, Kingscliffe, Northants, UK, ETO.

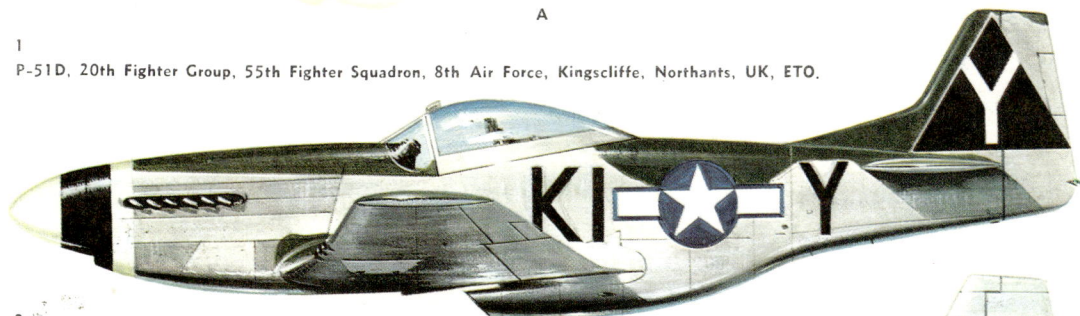

2
P-51D 20th Fighter Group, 79th Fighter Squadron, 8th Air Force, Kingscliffe, Northants, UK, ETO.
'Bridgets Bunnion'

3
P-51D, 359th Fighter Group, 368th Fighter Squadron, 8th Air Force, East Wretham, Norfolk, UK, ETO.
'Lady'

4
P-51D, 359th Fighter Group, 369th Fighter Squadron, 8th Air Force, East Wretham, Norfolk, UK, ETO.
'Hubert'

5
P-51D, 359th Fighter Group, 370th Fighter Squadron, 8th Air Force, East Wretham, Norfolk, UK, ETO.
'Daddys Girl'

6
P-51D, 356th Fighter Group, 359th Fighter Squadron, 8th Air Force, Martlesham, Suffolk, UK, ETO.

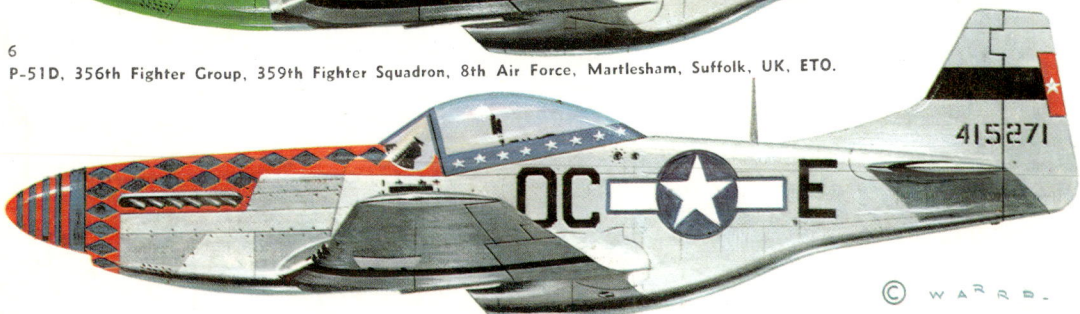

B

1
P-51D, 356th Fighter Group, 361st Fighter Squadron, 8th Air Force, Martlesham, Suffolk, UK, ETO.
'Jersey Jerk'

2
P-51D, 364th Fighter Group, 383rd Fighter Squadron, 8th Air Force, Hunington, Suffolk, UK, ETO.
'Babs in Arms'

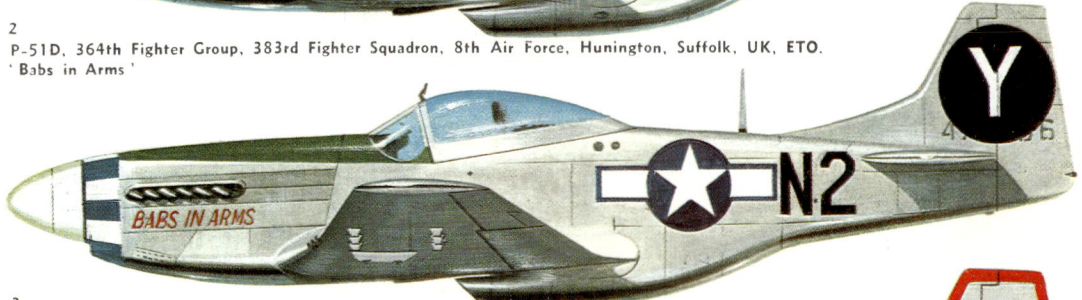

3
P-51D, 364th Fighter Group, 385th Fighter Squadron, 8th Air Force, Hunington, Suffolk, UK, ETO.
'Rugged Rebel.'

4
P-51D, 352nd Fighter Group, 328th Fighter Squadron, 8th Air Force, Bodney, Norfolk, UK, ETO.
'Straw Boss 2'

5
P-51D, 4th Fighter Group, 335th Fighter Squadron, 8th Air Force, Debden, Essex, UK, ETO.

6
P-51D, 355th Fighter Group, 354th Fighter Squadron, 8th Air Force, Steeple Morden, Herts, UK, ETO.
'Texas Terror IV'

C

1
P-51D, 355th Fighter Group, 357th Fighter Squadron, 8th Air Force, Steeple Morden, Herts, UK, ETO.

2
P-51D, 361st Fighter Group, 374th Fighter Squadron, 8th Air Force, Little Walden, Herts, UK, ETO.
'Duchess of Manhatten'

3
P-51D, 361st Fighter Group, 375th Fighter Squadron, 8th Air Force, Little Walden, Herts, UK, ETO.
'Lou IV'

4
-P-51D, 479th Fighter Group, 435th Fighter Squadron, 8th Air Force, Wattisham, Suffolk, UK, ETO.

5
P-51D, 55th Fighter Group, 338th Fighter Squadron, 8th Air Force, Wormingford, Northants, UK, ETO.
'Daquake'

6
P-51D, 55th Fighter Group, 343rd Fighter Squadron, 8th Air Force, Wormingford, Northants, UK, ETO.
'Miss Marilyn II'

D

1
P-51D, 339th Fighter Group, 503rd Fighter Squadron, 8th Air Force, Fowlmere, Cambs, UK, ETO.

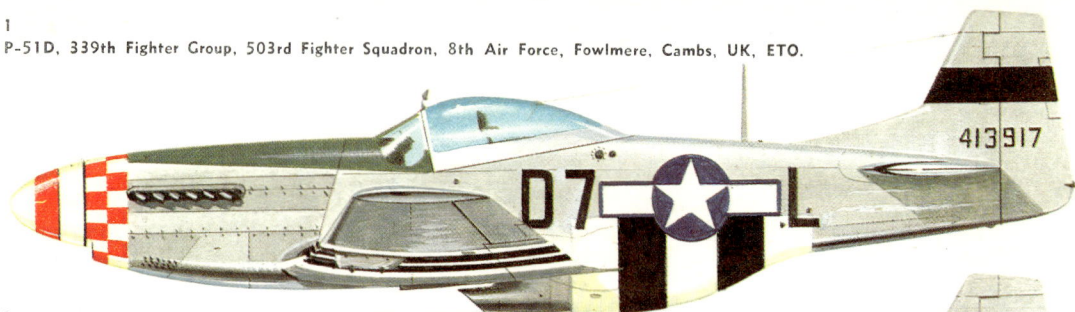

413917

D7 ★ L

2
P-51D, 339th Fighter Group, 504th Fighter Squadron, 8th Air Force, Fowlmere, Cambs, UK, ETO.
'Pauline'

414656

Pauline

6N ★ C

3
P-51D, 339th Fighter Group, 505th Fighter Squadron, 8th Air Force, Fowlmere, Cambs, UK, ETO.

413569

5Q ★ B

4
P-51D, 357th Fighter Group, 362nd Fighter Squadron, 8th Air Force, Leiston, Suffolk, UK, ETO.

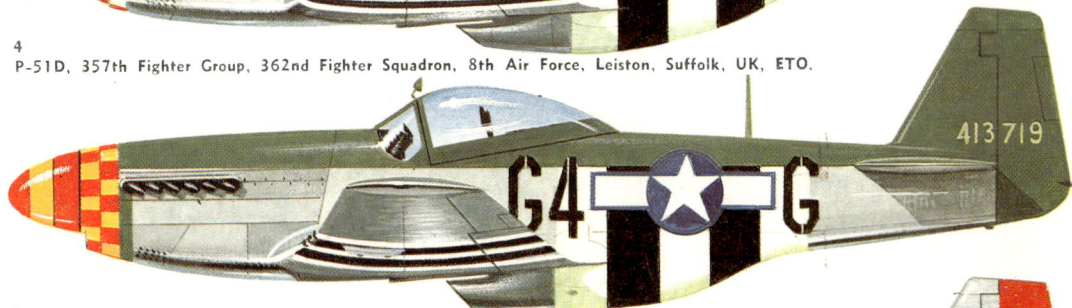

413719

G4 ★ G

5
P-51D 357th Fighter Group, 363rd Fighter Squadron, 8th Air Force, Leiston, Suffolk, UK, ETO.
'Old Crow'

414450

OLD CROW

B6 ★ S

6
P-51D, 357th Fighter Group, 364th Fighter Squadron, 8th Air Force, Leiston, Suffolk, UK, ETO.
'Tangerine'

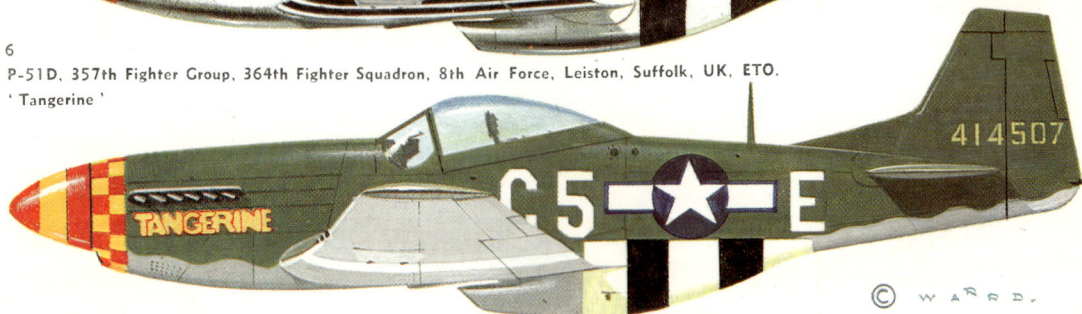

414507

TANGERINE

C5 ★ E

© WARD.

1

P-51D, 353rd Fighter Group, 350th Fighter Squadron, 8th Air Force, Raydon, Suffolk, UK, ETO.
'Galloping Ghost'

Galloping Ghost

LH ★ I

414673

2

P-51D, 353rd Fighter Group, 352nd Fighter Squadron, 8th Air Force, Raydon, Suffolk, UK, ETO.
'Donna-mite'

Donna-mite

SX ★ M

411624

3

P-51D, 78th Fighter Group, 82nd Fighter Squadron, 8th Air Force, Duxford, Cambs, UK, ETO.

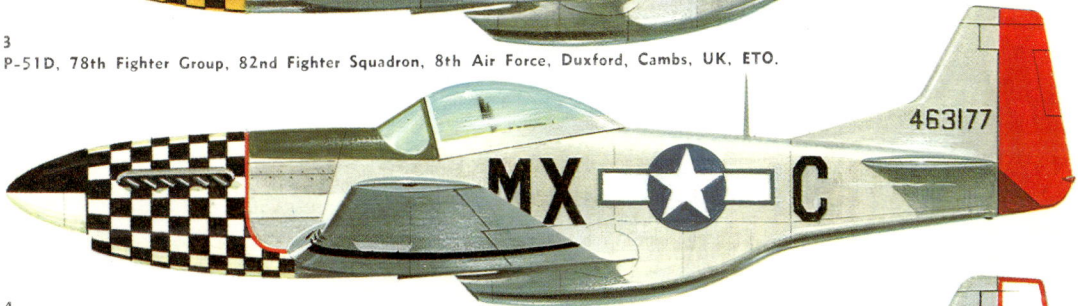

MX ★ C

463177

4

P-51D, 78th Fighter Group, 83rd Fighter Squadron, 8th Air Force, Duxford, Cambs, UK, ETO.
'Small Boy Here'

SMALL BOY HERE

HL ★ C

463620

5

P-51D, 78th Fighter Group, 84th Fighter Squadron, 8th Air Force, Duxford, Cambs, UK, ETO.

WZ ★ J

472163

6

F 6K, 69th Tactical Recon Group, 22nd Tactical Recon Squadron, 9th Air Force, ETO.

QL ★ L

412527

© WARD

1

P-51D, Unit unknown, ex 364th FG, 383rd FS, 8th AF, transferred to 9th Air Force, ETO.
'Babs in Arms'

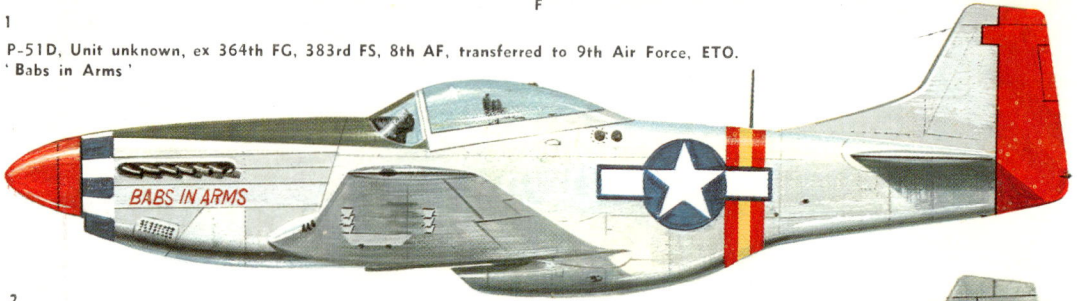

2

P-51D, Unit unknown, ex 354th Fighter Group, 9th Air Force, ETO.

3

P-51D, 370th Fighter Group, 402nd Fighter Squadron, 9th Air Force, ETO.
'Nancy Lee'

4

P-51D, 332nd Fighter Group, 100th Fighter Squadron, 15th Air Force, Italy.

5

P-51D, 31st Fighter Group, 307th Fighter Squadron, 15th Air Force, Mondolfo, Italy.
'American Beauty'

6

P-51D, 52nd Fighter Group, 4th Fighter Squadron, 15th Air Force, Madna, Italy.
'Queen Marjorie'

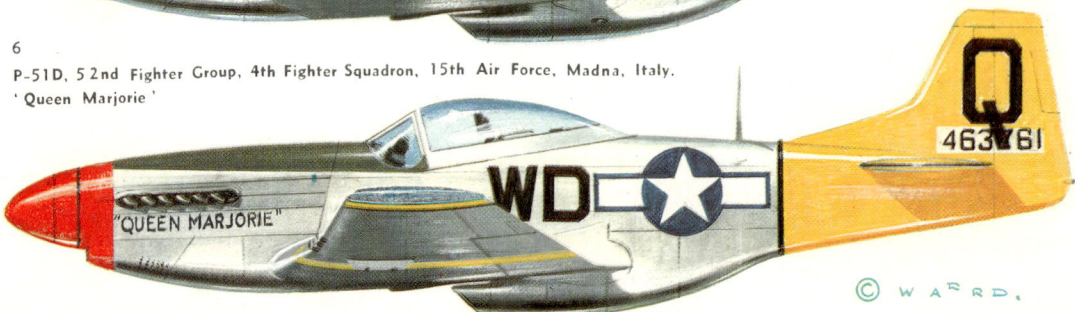

1
P-51D, 325th Fighter Group, 317th Fighter Squadron, HQ aircraft, 15th Air Force, Vincenzo, Italy.

2
P-51K, 311th Fighter Group, 529th Fighter Squadron, 10th Air Force, CBI.
'Shady Katy'

3
P-51K, 311th Fighter Group, 530th Fighter Squadron, 10th Air Force, CBI.
'Estelle'

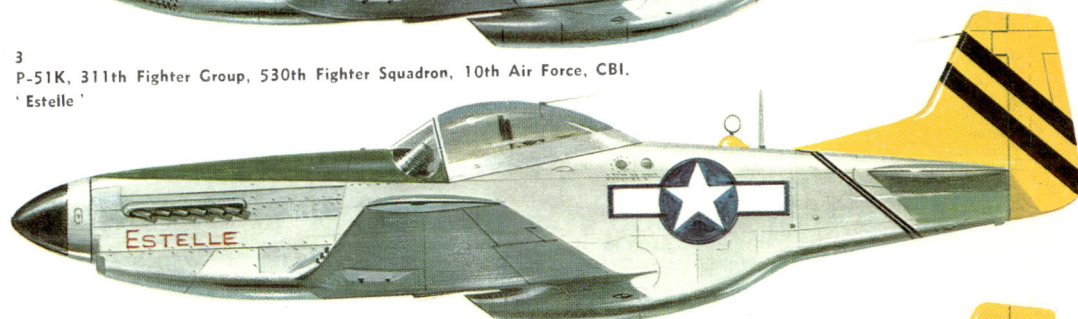

4
F-6K, 71st Tactical Recon Group, 82nd Tactical Recon Squadron, 5th Air Force, Philippines, POA.
'The Flying Undertaker'/'Snooks 5th'

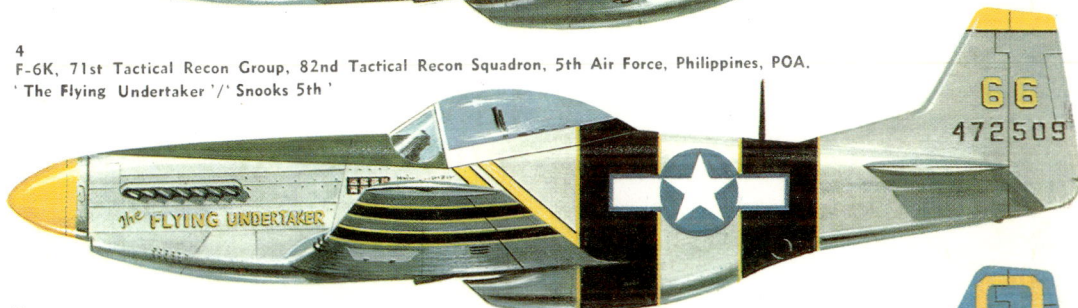

5
P-51D, Unit unknown, 5th Air Force, Philippines/Okinawa, POA.
'Jumpin-Jacques'

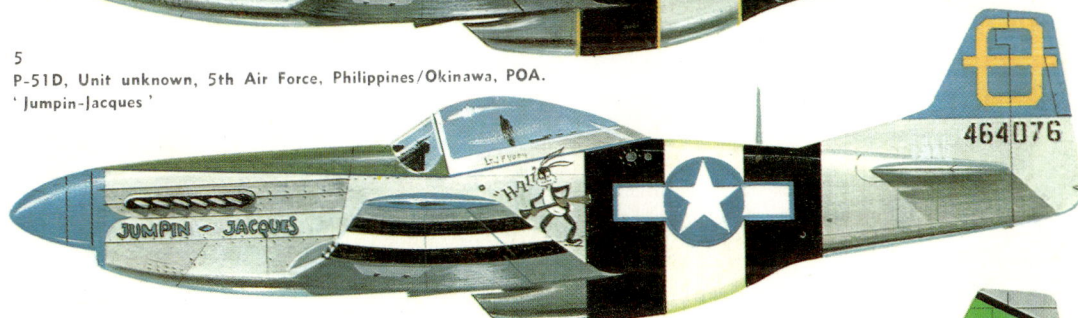

6
P-51D, 15th Fighter Group, 45th Fighter Squadron, VII Fighter Command, 20th Air Force, Iwo Jima, POA.

1
P-51D, 21st Fighter Group, 72nd Fighter Squadron, VII Fighter Command, 20th Air Force, Iwo Jima, POA.
'Little Angel '/' The 104 '

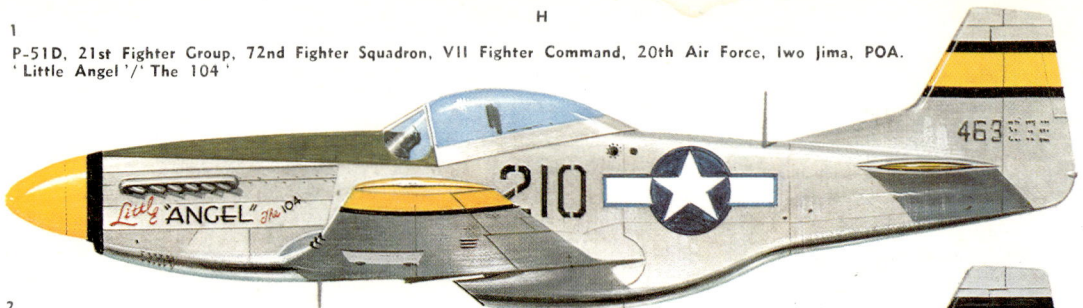

2
P-51D, 21st Fighter Group, 46th Fighter Squadron, VII Fighter Command, 20th Air Force, Iwo Jima, POA.

3
P-51D, 21st Fighter Group, 531st Fighter Squadron, VII Fighter Command, 20th Air Force, Iwo Jima, POA.

4
P-51D, 506th Fighter Group, 457th Fighter Squadron, VII Fighter Command, 20th Air Force, Iwo Jima, POA.
' Hel-eter '

5
P-51D, 506th Fighter Group, 458th Fighter Squadron, VII Fighter Command, 20th Air Force, Iwo Jima, POA.

6
P-51D, 506th Fighter Group, 459th Fighter Squadron, VII Fighter Command, 20th Air Force, Iwo Jima, POA.
' The Shawnee Princess '

'Babs in Arms,' ex 364th FG, 383rd FS, transferred to 9th AF, unit unknown. See colour illustration.

Above. F-6K of the 69th Tactical Recon Group, 22nd TRS, 9th AF, ETO. (via G. J. Letzter)

Below. Three F-6K's of the 69th TRG, QL- 22nd TRS, YC- 10th TRS, red spinner and tail marking. Photo taken at Speke. (USAF)

Checkertail P-51D of the 325th FG, 317th FS, 15th AF, flying over mountainous country in Italy. (via E. McDowell)

'Mary Nell' of the 325th FG, 317th FS, 15th AF, red nose, yellow wing bands inboard and at tip, yellow/black checks on tail. (E. McDowell)

'Dusty Butt,' 325th FG, 317th FS, 15th AF. Red nose, yellow wing tip and inboard bands. (via E. McDowell)

Above. 'Squeezie,' 325th
'Checkertail' FG, 319th FS, 15th
AF. Note yellow wing bands at
tip and inboard, red nose.
(E. McDowell)

Right. Close-up shot of P-51D
of the 325th FG, 317th FS, 15th
AF. Note wing tip yellow band
and absence of inboard band.
Red nose. (E. McDowell)

Below. P-51D, 325th FG, 318th
FS, with early tail marking.
Yellow wing bands, red nose.
(via E. McDowell)

Formation of P-51D's of the 31st FG, 308th FS, 15th AF, high over Italy. Red nose, red stripes on natural metal tail unit, yellow inboard wing bands, red/yellow wing tip. HL-C 'O Kaye' flown by Maj. Leland P. Molland, 11½ victories, CO of the 308th FS. HL-B flown by Capt. John J. Voll, 21 victories, see colour illustration. Note the codes of the 31st FG, 15th AF duplicate the codes of the 78th FG, 8th AF. 31st FG codes 307th FS, MX-; 308th FS, HL-; 309th FS, WZ-. (USAF)

P-51D's of the four 15th AF Fighter Groups, from top to bottom, HL-A, 31st FG, 308th FS; WD-Q, 52nd FG, 4th FS; 7, 100th FS; 00, 325th 'Checkertail' FG, personal mount of Lt.-Col. C. H. Beverley, 325th Group Commander. See colour illustrations. (USAF)

Red tailed 'Hel-eter' of the 506th FG, 457th FS, 20th AF, operating out of Iwo Jima escorting B-29 formations to Japan. Note twin radio masts aft of cockpit and extra mast under centre section.
(via G. J. Letzter)

P-51D of the 506th FG, 458th FS, 20th AF, Iwo Jima, Bonin Islands, July 1945. Black stripes on natural metal. (USAF)

Yellow tailed 'The Shawnee Princess' of the 506th FG, 462nd FS, 20th AF, Iwo Jima, Bonin Islands. (USAF)

Black striped P-51D of the 506th FG, 458th FS, 20th AF, parked alongside the runway against a background of volcanic dust blown up by the Merlins of other Mustangs taking off, Iwo Jima, July 1945. (USAF)

'Little Angel—the 104' of the 21st Fg, 72nd FS, 20th AF, yellow spinner, nose and tail stripe, after crash landing on Iwo Jima. Note fuel from fractured tank. (via G. J. Letzter)

Above. 'Lil Butch' of the 15th FG, 47th FS, 20th AF. Yellow/black/yellow spinner, Black tail marking, fuselage and wing bands outlined in yellow. Iwo Jima. (via G. J. Letzter)

Below. Formation of 15th FG, 45th FS, 20th AF, P-51D's, photo taken on B-29 escort mission to Japan. Iwo Jima. See colour illustration. (USAF)

Two P-51D's, 'Tiny Gay Babe' and 'Three of a Kind,' of the 21st FG, 72nd FS, 20th AF, on the parking area of an airfield on Iwo Jima, Bonin Islands. Yellow and black markings. (USAF)

Long line-up of P-51D's of the 15th FG, 78th FS, 20th AF, alongside the runway, Iwo Jima. Yellow and black markings. Note the Fighter Groups on Iwo Jima were units of the 7th AF under the Command of the 20th AF. (USAF)

Nose detail of F-6D 'The Flying Undertaker' /' Sooks-5th,' 71st TRG, 82nd TRS, 5th AF, POA. Flown by Maj. Wm. A. Shomo who on the 11th January 1945 whilst on a recon mission to Luzon in the Philippines intercepted a formation of 12 Japanese fighters escorting a Betty bomber. Attacking this force Capt. Shomo, as he then was, destroyed 6 fighters and the Betty. Lt. Paul Lipscomb, wingman, destroyed 3 fighters. For this action Maj. Shomo received the Congressional Medal of Honour and Lt. Lipscomb the Distinguished Flying Cross. (via G. J. Letzter)

Above. F-6D 'The Flying Undertaker,' 71st TRG, 82nd TRS, 5th AF, POA. See colour illustration. (via G. J. Letzter)

Starboard side nose detail of 'The Flying Undertaker,' yellow letters with black outline. Maj. Shomo was a licensed embalmer before joining the USAAF, hence the name of his aircraft!

Above. Black and white banded P-51D 'Jumpin-Jacques' flown by Lt. J. E. Young, unit unknown, 5th AF, POA. (via G. J. Letzter)

Right. Close-up showing detail of personal insignia of Lt. J. E. Young. (via G. J. Letzter)

Below. Okinawa based P-51D, unit unknown, 5th AF, POA. (via G. J. Letzter)

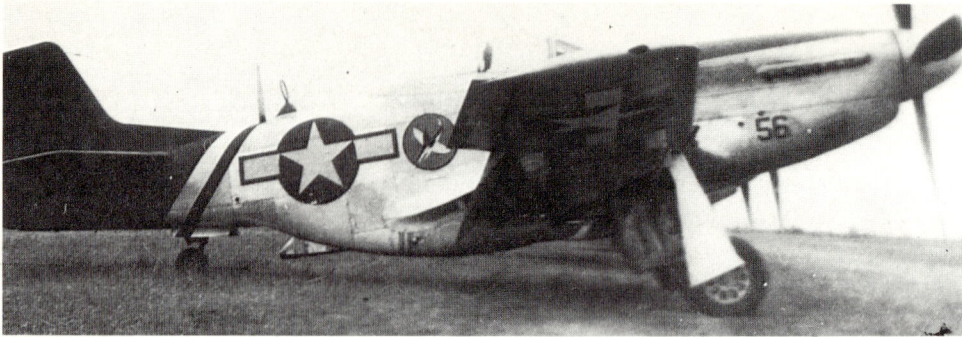

Black tailed P-51D of an unknown unit, 10th AF, CBI. Note DF loop. (Peter M. Bowers)

Black tail stripe and !, 84 and lightning flash on this P-51D, 2nd Air Commando Group, 10th AF, CBI. India 1945. Canopy OD. (Peter M. Bowers)

'My Ned,' a P-51K of the 311th FG, 530th FS, 10th AF, CBI. Yellow fin and rudder with black stripes, black fuselage stripes. Note DF loop ahead of radio mast. China 1945. (Peter M. Bowers)

P-51K 'Shady Katy' of the 311th FG, 529th FS, 10th AF, CBI. China 1945. (Peter M. Bowers)

'The Worldly Wench,' a P-51K of the 311th FG, 529th FS, 10th AF, CBI, note DF loop aft of radio mast. China 1945. (Peter M. Bowers)

P-51D's in very plain post-war finish, above PF-135, black 5, red spinner, below PF-267. (USAF)

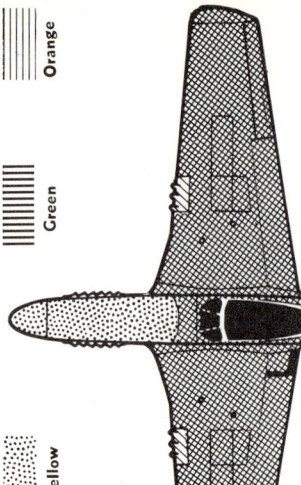

Orange

Green

Yellow

Medium Blue

White

Black

Red

Olive Drab

Bare Metal

Grey

C3 361st FG.
Standard yellow nose marking as in C2. Only Mustang Group to use medium blue as an upper surface camouflage. National marking on upper surface surrounded by narrow outline of bare metal, not shown on plan view.

C3 361st FG.
Under surface scheme showing D-Day Invasion stripes.

Note this plan view shows the standard position of the stripes but the position and sequence of colours varied on some aircraft, plainly shown on the side-view colour illustrations.

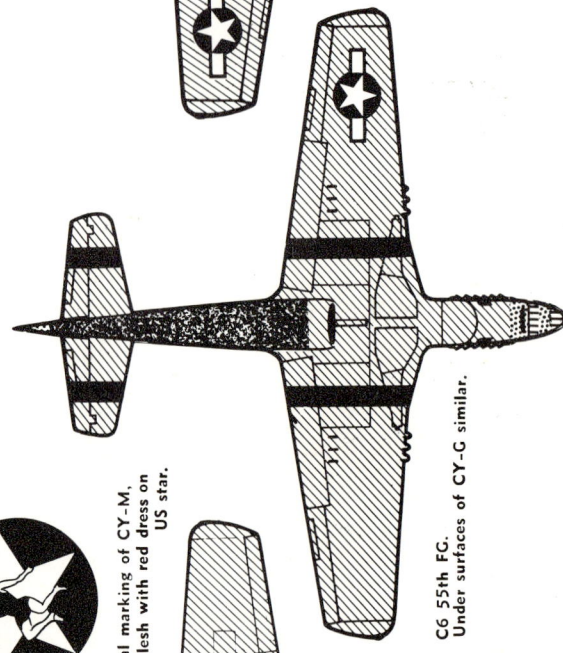

B6 355th FG.
Upper surface D-Day stripes and identity bands overpainted with temporary OD camouflage.

C6 55th FG.
Under surfaces of CY-G similar.

C6
Personal marking of CY-M, figure flesh with red dress on US star.

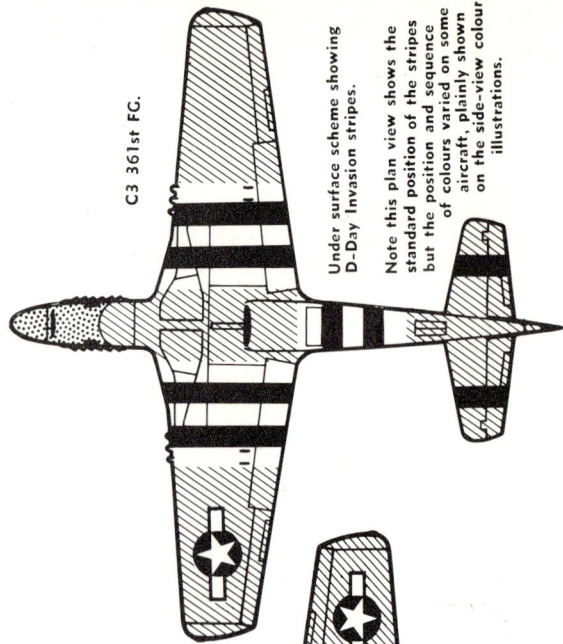

A1 20th FG.
Standard bare metal scheme applicable to all 8th AF P-51D's after addition of black identification bands.

KI-Y illustrated without bands subsequently painted on.

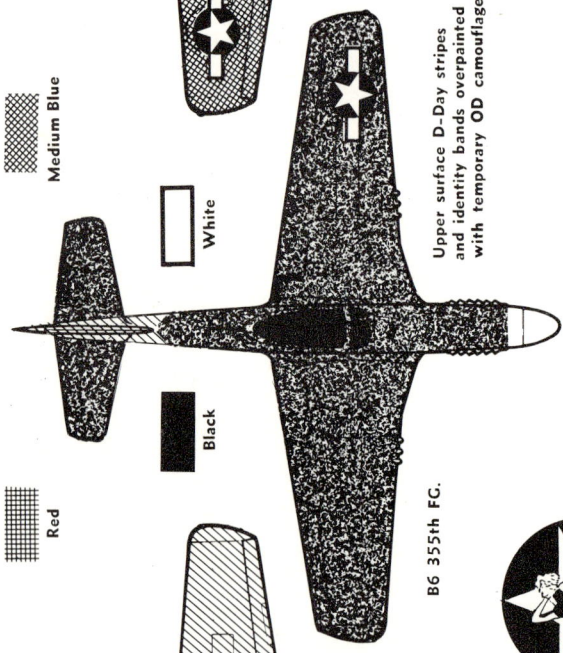

C6 55th FG.
Non-standard camouflage scheme apparently only applied to a/c of the 343rd FS. Upper surfaces of CY-G similar with addition of white tail bands.

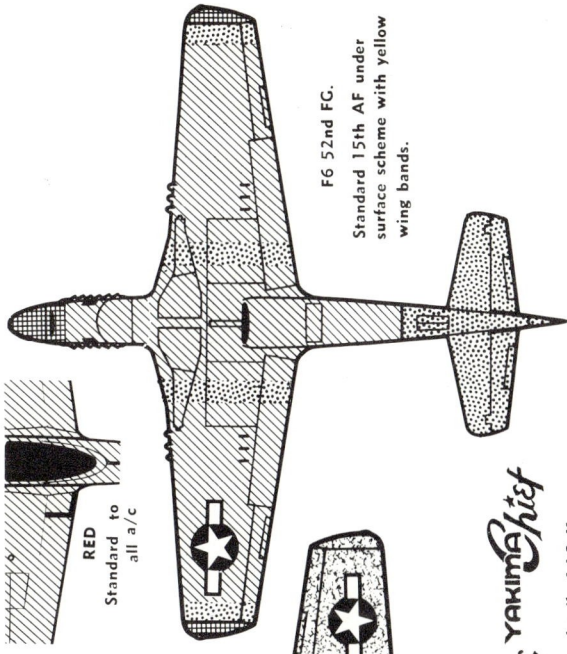

F6 52nd FG.
Standard 15th AF under surface scheme with yellow wing bands.

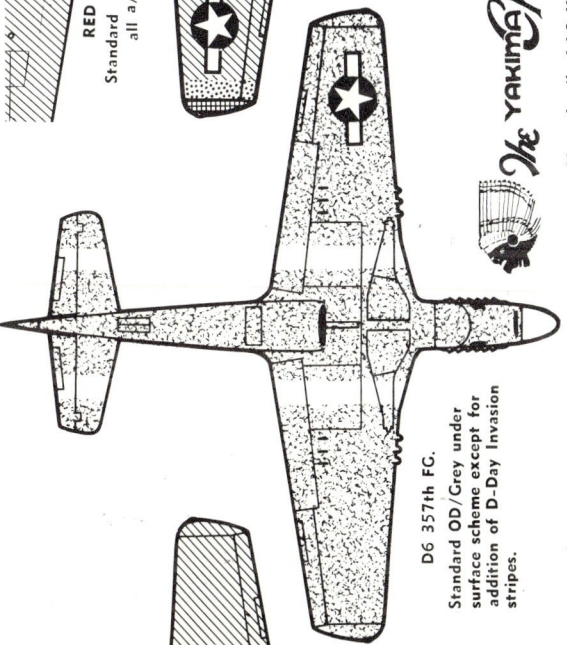

F6 52nd FG.
Upper surface scheme.

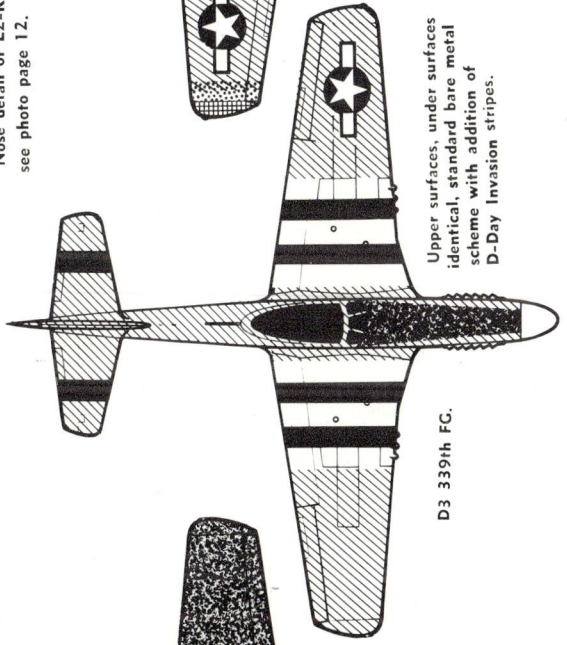

F6 52nd FG. wing tip

RED
Standard to all a/c

The Yakima Chief

Nose detail of L2-K, see photo page 12.

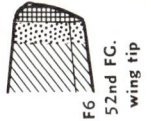

F6 52nd FG.

D6 357th FG.
Standard OD/Grey under surface scheme except for addition of D-Day Invasion stripes.

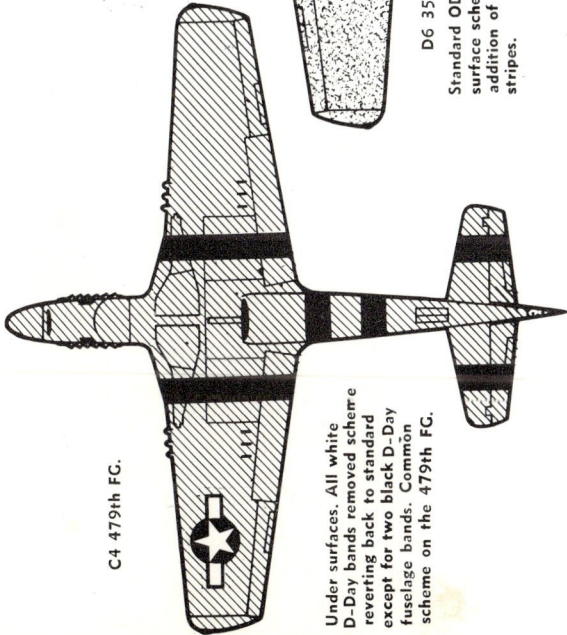

Upper surfaces, under surfaces identical, standard bare metal scheme with addition of D-Day Invasion stripes.

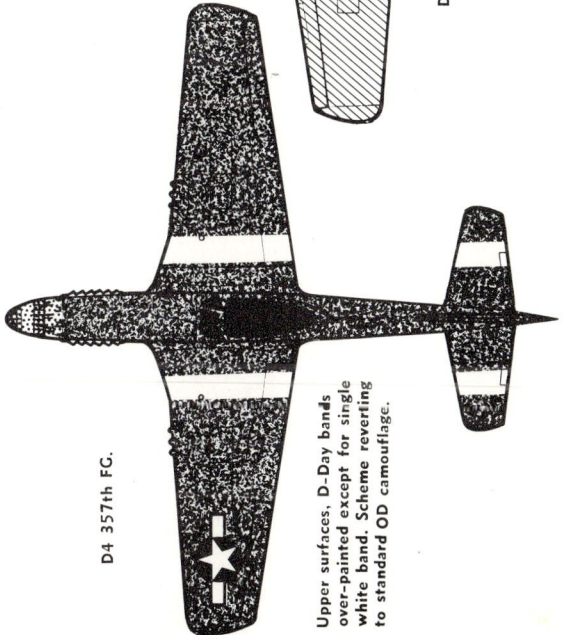

D3 339th FG.

C4 479th FG.
Under surfaces. All white D-Day bands removed scheme reverting back to standard except for two black D-Day fuselage bands. Common scheme on the 479th FG.

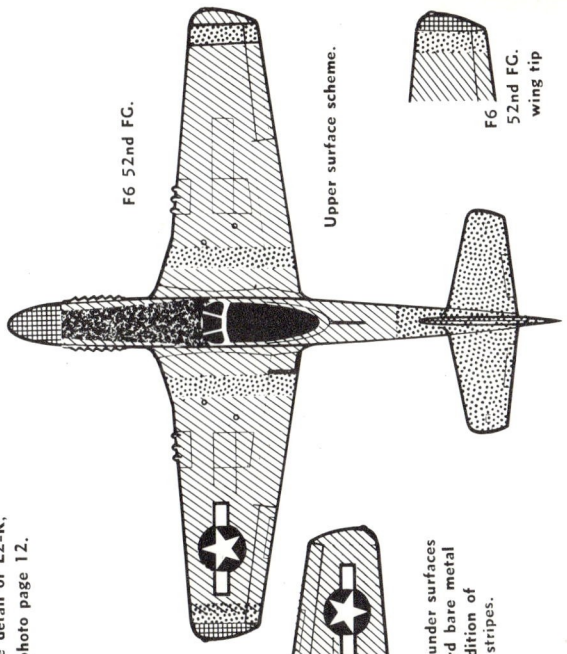

D4 357th FG.
Upper surfaces, D-Day bands over-painted except for single white band. Scheme reverting to standard OD camouflage.

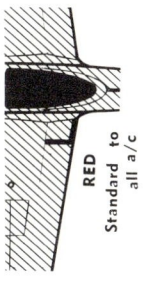

47

H5
506th FC.
458th FS. Iwo Jima, POA.

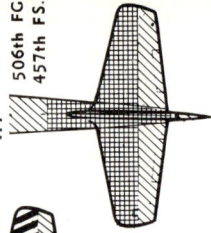

H4
506th FG.
457th FS.

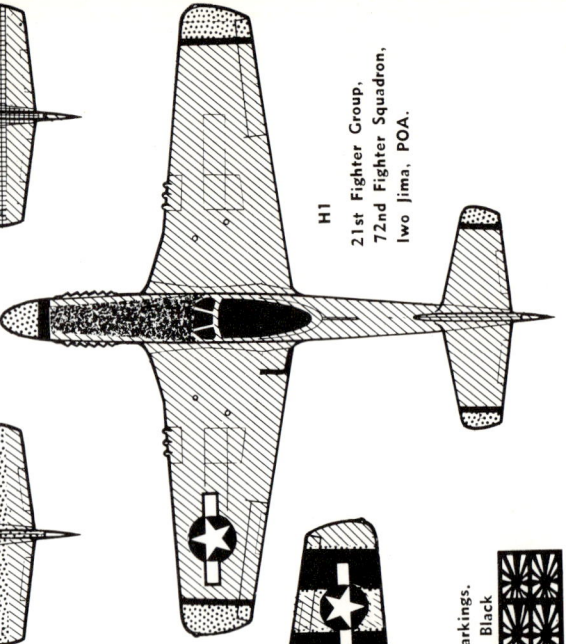

H1
21st Fighter Group,
72nd Fighter Squadron,
Iwo Jima, POA.

G6
15th FG. 45th FS
Iwo Jima, POA.

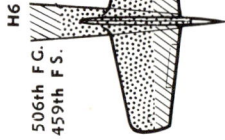

H6
506th FG.
459th FS.

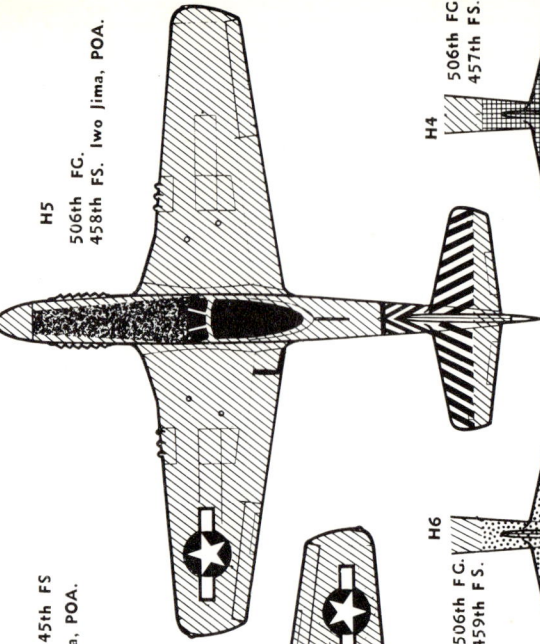

F5 Detail of
victory markings.

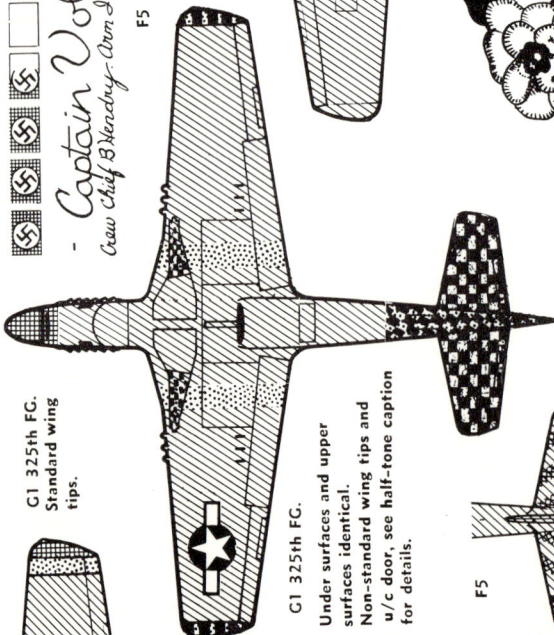

G4
victory markings.
Red on Black

Captain Voll
Crew Chief B.Hendry–Arn I.Sims

G4
F-6K, 71st Tactical Recon Group,
82nd Tactical Recon Squadron,
5th Air Force, Philippines, SWPA.
'The Flying Undertaker' /
'Snooks 5th'

F5
Detail of personal marking

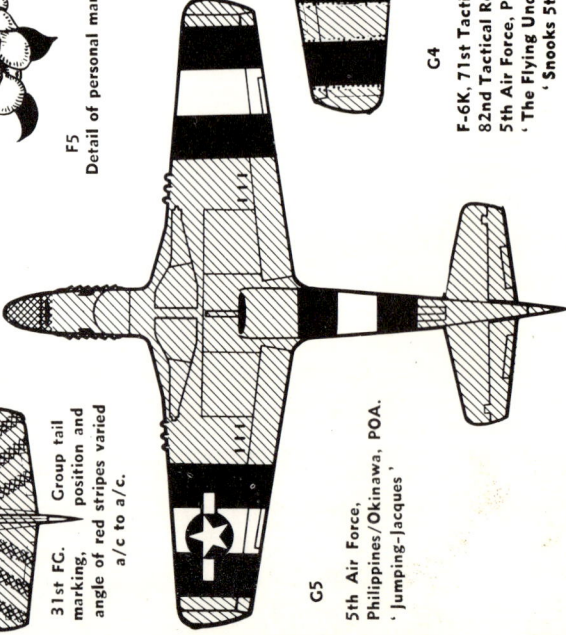

G1 325th FG.
Standard wing
tips.

G1 325th FG.
Under surfaces and upper
surfaces identical.
Non-standard wing tips and
u/c door, see half-tone caption
for details.

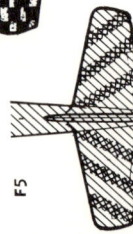

F5
31st FG.
Group tail
marking,
position and
angle of red stripes varied
a/c to a/c.

G5
5th Air Force,
Philippines/Okinawa, POA.
'Jumping-Jacques'

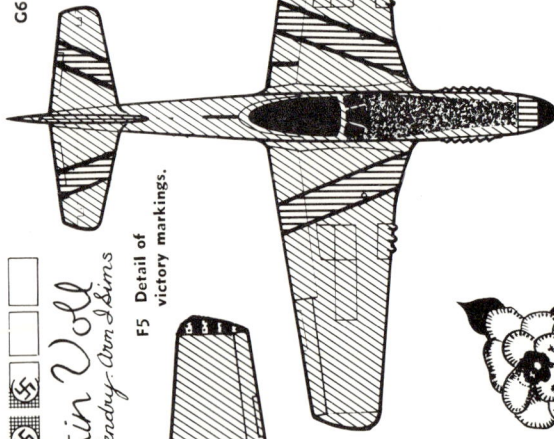

48

Colourful F-51D's of the Ohio Air National Guard 162nd Fighter Squadron. 1st a/c red/white/blue/yellow spinner; black 15; fuselage stripes, fin tip and tailplane tips red. 2nd a/c halved yellow/black spinner; black 64; red/white/blue fuselage stripes; fin and tailplane tips red. Black ONG on fuselage. (Ray E. Bowers)

Sharkmouth F-51D of the West Virginia Air National Guard more or less on the scrap heap, now a museum piece.

F-51D's of the Pennsylvania Air National Guard, 464103, above, yellow nose; black spinner, anti-glare and exhaust panel; yellow rudder; black fin tip. Note radio mast under centre-section. Below, 474624 with yellow spinner, fin and rudder top. Black anti-glare and exhaust panel and black tip to aft fuselage and rudder. Radio mast under centre-section. (via G. J. Letzter)

F-51D's in post-war scheme, FF-825 above and below with red rudder and red bar in national insignia. (USAF)

F-51D below FF-753, note large long-range tanks. (USAF)

Colourful F-51D's of the Ohio Air National Guard 162nd Fighter Squadron. 1st a/c red/white/blue/yellow spinner; black 15; fuselage stripes, fin tip and tailplane tips red. 2nd a/c halved yellow/black spinner; black 64; red/white/blue fuselage stripes; fin and tailplane tips red. Black ONG on fuselage. (Ray E. Bowers)

Sharkmouth F-51D of the West Virginia Air National Guard more or less on the scrap heap, now a museum piece.

F-51D's of the Pennsylvania Air National Guard, 464103, above, yellow nose; black spinner, anti-glare and exhaust panel; yellow rudder; black fin tip. Note radio mast under centre-section. Below, 474624 with yellow spinner, fin and rudder top. Black anti-glare and exhaust panel and black tip to aft fuselage and rudder. Radio mast under centre-section. (via G. J. Letzter)

F-51D's in post-war scheme, FF-825 above and below with red rudder and red bar in national insignia. (USAF)

F-51D below FF-753, note large long-range tanks. (USAF)